Eddie Cantor, Part 1 of 6

The Federal Bureau of Investigation (FBI)

The BiblioGov Project is an effort to expand awareness of the public documents and records of the U.S. Government via print publications. In broadening the public understanding of government and its work, an enlightened democracy can grow and prosper. Ranging from historic Congressional Bills to the most recent Budget of the United States Government, the BiblioGov Project spans a wealth of government information. These works are now made available through an environmentally friendly, print-on-demand basis, using only what is necessary to meet the required demands of an interested public. We invite you to learn of the records of the U.S. Government, heightening the knowledge and debate that can lead from such publications.

Included are the following Collections:

Budget of The United States Government
Presidential Documents
United States Code
Education Reports from ERIC
GAO Reports
History of Bills
House Rules and Manual
Public and Private Laws

Code of Federal Regulations
Congressional Documents
Economic Indicators
Federal Register
Government Manuals
House Journal
Privacy act Issuances
Statutes at Large

FEDERAL BUREAU OF INVESTIGATION

FREEDOM OF INFORMATION/PRIVACY ACTS SECTION

COVER SHEET

SUBJECT: EDDIE CANTOR

FILE NUMBER: 62-26544

SUBJECT   Eddie Cantor

FBI FILE # 62- 26944

62-26644-6

Eddie Cantor

Dr. Cantor examines Uncle Sam

(Eddie Cantor's radio sketch for which Chase & Sanborn have had the greatest number of requests.)

•

EDDIE CANTOR, D.D. (*Depression Doctor*) was sitting in his office on the Chase and Sanborn Hour one Sunday night, when a knock was heard outside the door and a weak voice asked, "Where's a doc?"

"Right here, my friend," said Eddie. "Sit down in that chair, open up your collar and say 'aaah'."

"Me no can say."

"Well why can't you say 'aaah'?"

"Sorry, doc, me no speaka English."

"Well then, say 'aaah' in your own language."

"Booh."

"Good. Now say 'booh' in your language."

"Aaah."

"That's it. Let's have a look. Your tonsils are very low. You should wear arch supports."

"You think I'm gonna live, doc?"

"Well, your chances are 9 to 1," replied Eddie. And sure enough it was right on the doctor's card. Dr. Cantor—9 to 1.

"There is another patient outside," said Jimmy Wallington, who had been watching the proceedings with interest.

"Come in my good man," said Dr. Cantor.

In strode a tall benevolent man, with red striped trousers, white chin whiskers and a high blue hat with white stars. "Don't you know me?" he said. "I'm Uncle Sam."

Eddie looked at him a moment and shook his head. "Yes, you are my Uncle Sam all right, but you have changed. You look very thin. Have you done any eating lately . . . you know, food?"

Uncle Sam sadly shook his head. "You see, Eddie, I have a lot of nephews and nieces out of work . . ."

"I understand," said Eddie, "you don't like to sponge on them. I'm going to ask you a few questions, Uncle Sam. When were you born?"

"On July 4, 1776."

"That makes you a hundred and fifty-five years old. Why, you're just a kid, Uncle. You are suffering from growing pains, that's all."

"Maybe," said Uncle Sam weakly, "but I feel terrible."

"Don't be foolish, Uncle Sam, I have been sicker than you myself." Eddie was rapidly unbuttoning his coat and vest. "Look Uncle, did I ever show you my operation? Oooh, was I sick. And look at me now. Don't worry, you will feel better soon. You have had these attacks before. Remember—1907 . . . 1893?"

"Yes, but this is the worst one yet."

"No, no, no," said Eddie. "That's what you say every time. Why, compared to that internal trouble you had in 1865 which nearly upset your whole system, you haven't even got a bad cold now. Your blood pressure is a little too low and your temperature is below normal but everything will go up soon; the worst is over, Uncle Sam."

The kindly old man shook his head. "That may be," he moaned, "but I never felt worse."

Eddie smiled and patted him on the back. "Let me tell you something, Uncle Sam. The time you were really sick was late in 1928 and during '29. That's when you thought you were feeling fine but you were really running a high fever. You were suffering from enlargement of the spendiorum, speculationitis, and inflationary rheumatism. And you didn't even know it. It looks to me, Uncle Sam—as if you spent 1929 under the influence of intoxicating ideas. You got a drink of that Wall Street cocktail . . . you went up like a rocket and came down like a stick."

"Wall Street cocktail?"

"Sure—one drink and you get a seat on the curb with your feet in the gutter. That's what was wrong with you in 1929. But you didn't get a headache until 1931."

"How do you explain that, Eddie?"

"That's simple. In 1929 you went on a spree, in 1930 you had to be put to bed and 1931 was the morning after the year before. But now, do what I tell you. Keep cheerful. Get out of the shadows and into the sunshine. Face the sun and the shadows will fall behind you. If you think you are in the soup, get acquainted with the people who would thank God if they could get a bowl of soup into them. You've got plenty of assets, Uncle Sam. You've got a country with 350 billion dollars . . . you've got mountains full of gold and silver and any time you need a little pocket money, just go over and break off a piece of mountain. You've got the biggest factory in the world for building happy homes . . . Niagara Falls. But the place I want you to visit especially is the Grand Canyon . . . the biggest, deepest, widest place to drop all your troubles and start off fresh for 1932."

Printed in U. S. A.

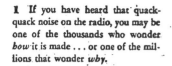

1 If you have heard that quack-quack noise on the radio, you may be one of the thousands who wonder *how* it is made . . . or one of the millions that wonder *why*.

2 This making quackee is like making whoopee. It's an old American custom. Even when it was new it was an old American custom.

3 To make quack-quack successfully, you use every part of the body, except the nose. The size or shape of the nose positively does not matter. George Jessel can make quackee just as well as Cantor.

7 Expel the air abruptly from the mouth. One man says let it come out like the geyser in Yellowstone Park. Of course the geyser really isn't in Yellowstone Park . . . he's chopping wood in Holland!

8 On the first quack, you may not have the right pitch or volume. If at first you don't succeed keep practising until you make a perfect goose of yourself.

9 If you are still unsuccessful, catch a goose and observe how quack-quack is made. Wives can learn other lessons from the goose, which is considered foolish because it thinks about its fine feathers and forgets the big bill.

4 An ear for music is fairly important. But you don't need *much* ear. Even if you have no more than Rubinoff there is still hope.

5 The mouth, of course, is most important. . . . After moistening the lips, hold them tightly together, like you do when your wife asks for a new hat.

6 Roll the eyes to the right . . . reverse . . . and roll them to the left. We used to roll them just to the right . . . The reverses are on account of the depression. Please master this trick for yourself. I can't roll your eyes for you. Each person must roll his own.

10 Once you learn to make quackquacks, press the forehead and chin together so your success won't swell your head. Of course the swelling may go elsewhere. Policemen wear large shoes because their success goes to their feet.

11 Once you have learned to quack, do it in public. Then things will begin to come your way . . . especially vegetables . . . You will find that potatoes and tomatoes are cheaper this way . . . and it is no hardship to have people throw tomatoes at you unless . . .

12 . . . somebody forgets to take them out of the can!

JEH:HW   February 1, 1935.

                          Time-10:42 A.M.

          MEMORANDUM FOR MR. TAMM

          During a telephonic conversation, ▮▮▮▮▮▮▮
mentioned that Mr. McIntyre of the White House had
sent over to the Department a telegram which he had
received from Eddie Cantor asking for various
information on the subject of "Crime" in order to
prepare for a radio broadcast in this connection.

          ▮▮▮▮▮▮▮ stated that he was routing the
telegram to me with the idea that I might be able
to furnish some information in regard to the Division.
I stated that I would be glad to do this.

                    Very truly yours,

                    John Edgar Hoover,
                    Director.

     1 copy

b7C

RECORDED
&
INDEXED

FILES SECTION
MAILED
★ FEB 2 1935 ★
P. M.
DIVISION OF INVESTIGATION,
U. S. DEPARTMENT OF JUSTICE

62- 26544 -1
DIVISION OF INVESTIGATION
FEB - 4 1935
U. S. DEPARTMENT JUSTICE

February 4, 1935.

RECORDED 62-26544-2

Mr. Eddie Cantor,
Columbia Broadcasting Company,
485 Madison Avenue,
New York, New York.

Dear Mr. Cantor:

Mr. Marvin McIntyre, Assistant Secretary to the President, has requested that I furnish you the information requested in your telegram of January 31.

I regret that I have very little information along the lines in which you are interested, that is, the number of police officers killed yearly in performance of duty, average salary of a policeman and other such statistics. The following information was given in an article published in the September, 1933, issue of "Police 13-13", the publication of the Chicago Police Department. It quoted as its source of information, a recent number of the "Monthly Labor Review", issued by the United States Department of Labor. The lowest salary paid by a Metropolitan Police Department is the $840 per year paid the senior patrolman in Mobile, Alabama. The highest schedule is found in New York City and Los Angeles, California where a senior patrolman receives $3,000 per year. A Mobile detective receives $900 a year, while a New York detective receives $4,000. Other cities are quoted as follows:

	Senior Patrolman	Detective	Police Sergeant
Chicago, Illinois	$1,967		$2,282
Detroit, Michigan	1,928	$1,928	2,073
Kansas City, Missouri	1,800	2,100	2,100
Newark, New Jersey	2,500		3,000
Portland, Maine	1,643		1,823
Savannah, Georgia	1,458	1,654	1,656
St. Paul, Minnesota	1,758	2,058	1,884
Yonkers, New York	2,750	3,200	3,400

The above information is, of course, based entirely upon the figures quoted by "Police 13-13", in 1933.

I have just received a copy of the Year Book of the Scranton, Pennsylvania Police Department, and find it gives police officers' salaries for that city as $3,000 for the Superintendent, who is the highest paid man in the Department, and $2,160 for patrolmen. These salaries are subject to a 10% economy reduction.

The 1935 World Almanac quotes the following salaries for the New York Police Department, as of October 24, 1934, but states actually smaller salaries are being paid during the economy regime: captains $5,000, lieutenants $4,000, sergeants $3,500, patrolmen $2,000 to $3,000, policewomen and patrolwomen $2,000 to $3,000.

I regret that I do not have any reports or estimates giving the number of officers killed in the line of duty.

As of possible interest to you, I am inclosing a copy of the address given by the Attorney General, and the address which I gave during the Attorney General's Conference on Crime, held in Washington during December, 1934. I am also inclosing the following publications of this Division which deal, of course, only with its law enforcement and identification activities:

Uniform Crime Reports - Third Quarterly Bulletin, 1934
The War on Crime
Fingerprints
The Work and Functions of the Division of Investigation
The Division of Investigation
Interesting Latent Fingerprint Cases
Training of Personnel

Sincerely yours,

John Edgar Hoover,
Director.

Incl. #803254.

2 copies
c-1 Mr. Marvin McIntyre

eb;eh;gjrm   February 4, 1935.

62-26544-2

Hon. Marvin McIntyre,
Assistant Secretary to the President,
The White House,
Washington, D. C.

Dear Mr. McIntyre:

Your memorandum of January 31 with
which you attached a copy of a telegram received
from Mr. Eddie Cantor, requesting information regarding police, was directed to me.

I have today sent to Mr. Cantor such
information as I have available along with various
publications dealing with the work of this Division.

A copy of my letter to Mr. Cantor is
inclosed.

With my best wishes and kind regards,
I am

Sincerely yours,

Inclosure.

HENRY SUYDAM
Special Assistant to the Attorney General.

Department of Justice
Washington

February 1, 1935.

MEMORANDUM FOR MR. J. EDGAR HOOVER,
DIRECTOR OF THE DIVISION OF INVESTIGATION.

     Attached is the memorandum of Mr. McIntyre.
If we can furnish Mr. Cantor with proper information
he ought to be able to do an effective broadcast. I
suggest sending him copies of any of your speeches
that you think would be helpful in such a broadcast,
together with the pamphlets describing the work and
functions of the Division of Investigation and any
other material that you think would be appropriate.

Henry Suydam

Henry Suydam,
Special Assistant to the Attorney General.

RECORDED

62-26544-2

DIVISION OF INVESTIGATION

FEB 6 1935

FEB 14 1935

Let. to Mr. Eddie
Cantor 2/4/35
EB

Let. to Mr. McIntyre
2/4/35
EB

COPIES DESTROYED
70 AUG 11 1964

THE WHITE HOUSE
WASHINGTON

January 31, 1935.

MEMORANDUM FOR: Department of Justice.

What may I advise Mr. Cantor?

H. H. McINTYRE.

RECORDED

FEB 15 1935

FEB 14 1935

FEB 19 1935

G

COPY

TELEGRAM   THE WHITE HOUSE
WASHINGTON.

14 PO. RA. 59- D. L. 11+15 a.m.

Washington, D. C., January 31, 1935.

Marvin McIntyre.

It was nice seeing you again and meeting your charming
daughter. Am anxious to do a broadcast on Crime Asking
America to cooperate with the Police. Can you send me
information as to how many policemen are killed each year
during performance of their duty, average salary of policeman,
etc. I would appreciate it greatly. Kindest regards,

                    Eddie Cantor.

RECORDED 61-26544-2

FEB 18 1935

FEB 15 1935

TOLSON   BACKUS

jeh;bw

FEDERAL BUREAU OF INVESTIGATION
UNITED STATES DEPARTMENT OF JUSTICE

TO: COMMUNICATIONS SECTION.   June 11, 1938.

Transmit the following message to:

RECORDED

62-26544-3

EDDIE CANTOR

BEVERLY HILLS, CALIFORNIA.

I HAVE READ YOUR WIRE TO MISTER HOOVER WHO IS IN FLORIDA STOP HE ASKS ME

TO SAY TO YOU THAT HE DEEPLY APPRECIATES YOUR FINE MESSAGE AND SINCERELY

REGRETS HIS INABILITY TO APPEAR UPON THE PROGRAM BECAUSE OF THE UNCERTAINTY

OF COMMITMENTS AND PLANS IN CONNECTION WITH FORTHCOMING TRIAL OF THE KIDNAPER

OF THE CASH BOY STOP HE REQUESTS THAT I GIVE YOU HIS VERY BEST REGARDS AND

ALL GOOD WISHES STOP

                        HELEN GANDY
                   Secretary to Mr. J. Edgar Hoover.

FEDERAL BUREAU OF INVESTIGATION.
U. S. DEPARTMENT OF JUSTICE
COMMUNICATIONS SECTION
JUN 11 1938
WESTERN UNION

SENT VIA

11 1964

FEDERAL BUREAU OF INVESTIGATION,
U. S. DEPARTMENT OF JUSTICE

COMMUNICATIONS SECTION

JUN 11 1938

WESTERN UNION

LONG WH3 80 NL 2 EXTRA

TDS BEVERLYHILLS CALIF JUN 10

J EDGAR HOOVER

WASHDC

CONGRATULATIONS IT GOES WITHOUT SAYING THAT ANY MESSAGE FROM

YOU ON CRIME IS TAKEN SERIOUSLY BY ALL AMERICA. CAN YOU

AND WILL YOU APPEAR ON MY RADIO PROGRAM FROM LOSANGELES ON JUNE

TWENTIETH DAY AFTER FATHERS DAY AND DELIVER A SHORT

MESSAGE REGARDING A CLOSER RELATIONSHIP BETWEEN FATHERS AND SONS AS

ONE MEANS OF CRIME PREVENTION. I WOULD BE HAPPY TO MAKE A SUBSTANTIAL

CONTRIBUTION TO THE FUND FOR G MENS WIDOWS. PLEASE WIRE

ME IMMEDIATELY KINDEST REGARDS

EDDIE CANTOR BEVERLYHILLS CALIF.

808A.

RECORDED
&
INDEXED.

62-26544-3

FEDERAL BUREAU OF INVESTIGATION

JUN 13 1938

Director
Federal Bureau of Investigation   **PERSONAL AND**
Washington, D. C.   **CONFIDENTIAL**

Dear Sir:

In a recent conversation with ████████████
National Broadcasting Company of Hollywood, California, he
being a director and producer of shows, he advised me that
JACK BENNY, radio comedian, who, according to today's press,
pled guilty to smuggling charges in New York City, has been
████████████ as to the outcome of the trial. ████████████
████████████████████ is intimately acquainted with him.
BENNY and his sponsors were very much afraid that he would receive a penitentiary sentence in connection with this case.

He advised me confidentially that EDDIE CANTOR,
who has recently made a number of public remarks relative to
his dislike for HITLER and things German in general, has had
difficulty with his sponsors, the American Tobacco Company,
and the sponsor actually endeavored to cancel his contract
after a recent episode in Hollywood. They were not legally
able to break this contract and the comedian has eight or nine
weeks before it expires.

After the conclusion of a recent broadcast in
Hollywood, CANTOR made some remarks about HITLER and an individual in the rear of the studio arose and left and was followed by two persons, who are reported to have attacked him
after engaging in a verbal dispute outside the studio. There
was some talk of filing charges against the attackers, one of
whom was said to have been an individual on the program with
CANTOR. Apparently the incident, as well as CANTOR'S remarks,
were very disgusting to the broadcasting company officials
and he is becoming increasingly unpopular in radio circles.

Very truly yours,   62-26544-4

RECORDED
&
INDEXED   R. B. HOOD,
RBH:MO   Special Agent in Charge

LBN:LCB   May 6, 1940

RECORDED 65-26544-5

Mr. Eddie Cantor
c/o Columbia Broadcasting System
485 Madison Avenue
New York, New York

Dear Mr. Cantor:

I listened to the citizens program which
was held at Skelly's Stadium at the University
of Tulsa with a great deal of interest and I
was particularly impressed with your remarks
regarding citizenship. I think that those of
us who are privileged to speak from time to time
should never let an opportunity pass without
discussing the obligations of citizenship and
the absolute necessity of doing everything we
can to perpetuate the American principles of
Life, Liberty and the Pursuit of Happiness.

I appreciated very much indeed the kind
references to the statement which I recently
made in an address and, of course, it was a
real source of encouragement to hear that you
thought we had done our job well. This, I can
assure you, has been our goal for years and
I trust that we may continue to merit your
approbation.

With best wishes and kind regards,

Sincerely yours,

J. Edgar Hoover

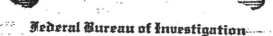

Federal Bureau of Investigation
United States Department of Justice
Washington, D. C.

LBN:LCB   May 6, 1940

MEMORANDUM FOR MR. TOLSON

    Eddie Cantor in his broadcast from Skelly's Stadium, University of Tulsa on Sunday evening, May 5th, over WMAL after referring to his friendship with Will Rogers and the obligations of citizenship, quoted the Director to the effect that if we used our heads today, we will not have to use our battleships, etc. tomorrow. Mr. Cantor then pointed out that the Director speaks from experience because he has been confronted with the job of meeting with the enemies from within and "he has done that job well." This statement was followed, as you will recall, by considerable applause. Mr. Cantor then went on to say if we used our heads we can make America what it should be.

    A note is attached to Mr. Cantor.

Respectfully,

L. B. Nichols

RECORDED & ~~INDEXED~~

62-26544-5

FEDERAL BUREAU OF INVESTIGATION

3   MAY 11 1940

U.S. DEPARTMENT OF JUSTICE

TOLSON

LHW:RC

URGENT   November 9, 1943

To: COMMUNICATIONS SECTION.

SAC LOS ANGELES

Transmit the following message to:

PLEASE DELIVER THE FOLLOWING MESSAGE IMMEDIATELY, TO:

62-26544-6

RECORDED

Mr. Eddie Cantor
1012 North Roxbury Drive
Beverly Hills, California

DEAR EDDIE: I APPRECIATED YOUR WIRE OF THE EIGHTH. THERE IS NO QUESTION BUT THAT ONE OF THE GREAT DOMESTIC PROBLEMS TODAY IS THE SHOCKING INCREASE IN THE NUMBER OF YOUTHFUL OFFENDERS. THE FIRST SIX MONTHS OF THIS YEAR WITNESSED A EIGHT NINE POINT FIVE PER CENT INCREASE IN THE ARREST AND FINGERPRINTING OF GIRLS UNDER TWENTY-ONE YEARS OF AGE FOR OFFENSES AGAINST COMMON DECENCY. SUCH OFFENSES INCLUDE DRUNKENNESS, VAGRANCY, DISORDERLY CONDUCT, PROSTITUTION, AND COMMERCIALIZED VICE. THE ARRESTS AND FINGERPRINTING OF GIRLS UNDER TWENTY-ONE INCREASED THIRTY PER CENT FOR CRIMES AGAINST PROPERTY FOR THE FIRST SIX MONTHS OF THIS YEAR. SUCH CRIMES ARE ROBBERY, BURGLARY, THEFT, LARCENY AND RELATED OFFENSES. ARRESTS OF BOYS AND GIRLS, AGE SEVENTEEN, INCREASED SEVENTEEN POINT SEVEN PERCENT, AND FOR ALL AGES, UNDER EIGHTEEN, ARRESTS OF BOYS AND GIRLS INCREASED THIRTEEN POINT SIX PERCENT. THESE FIGURES ARE AGGRAVATED BY THE FACT THAT THOUSANDS OF BOYS AGED EIGHTEEN ARE IN THE ARMY AND IN SOME INSTANCES BOYS UNDER EIGHTEEN ARE PRODUCTIVELY EMPLOYED WHICH WOULD NOT BE THE CASE IN OTHER YEARS. MORE PERSONS AGED EIGHTEEN WERE ARRESTED IN THE FIRST SIX MONTHS THIS YEAR, AS WAS THE CASE IN NINETEEN FORTY-TWO, THAN IN ANY OTHER AGE GROUP. THEY WERE FOLLOWED BY THE SEVENTEEN AND NINETEEN YEAR OLDS. OUR YOUTH IS BLAMED FOR THIS SORDID PICTURE BUT THE REAL FAULT LIES ON THE SHOULDERS OF THE ADULTS. WARTIME CONDITIONS HAVE BROUGHT ON DISLOCATIONS AND INCREASED,

(continued)

Mr. E. A. Tamm
Mr. Clegg
Mr. Coffey
Mr. Glavin
Mr. Ladd
Mr. Nichols
Mr. Rosen
Mr. Tracy
Mr. Acers
Mr. Harbo
Mr. Hendon
Mr. McGuire
Mr. Mumford
Mr. Piper
Mr. Quinn Tamm
Mr. Nease
Miss Gandy

5:00 PM   Per

RECORDED COPY FILED IN 62-26235-2124

THAN DECREASED, THE RESPONSIBILITIES OF PARENTS, MANY OF WHOM

THEIR CHILDREN TO SHIFT FOR THEMSELVES WHILE THEY FILL LUCRATIVE

ONS. IN MANY SUCH INSTANCES, CHILDREN OF NEGLECTFUL PARENTS ARE

D ON BY THE SPIRIT OF WARTIME ABANDON WHICH AFFECTS YOUNG AND OLD

ND QUESTIONABLE THRILLS AND UNWHOLESOME AMUSEMENT IN DEGRADING

WITH UNFIT COMPANIONS. THAT, FOR MANY, IS THE START DOWN THE

O RUIN. PARENTS OF AMERICA MUST DISCHARGE THE SACRED TRUST IMPOSED

MOLDING OF YOUNG LIVES, AND WE CANNOT AFFORD TO DISSIPATE

OW'S GOOD CITIZENSHIP BY NEGLECTING TODAY'S YOUNGSTERS.

ES, SCHOOLS, CIVIC GROUPS, AND LAW ENFORCEMENT MUST JOIN WITH

A'S AROUSED PARENTS IN ATTACKING AND SOLVING THIS MOST PRESSING

M. WE MUST GIVE OUR YOUNGSTERS WHOLESOME PROGRAMS OF ACTIVITY

ACH THEM IDEALS WHICH ARE THE FOUNDATION OF GOOD CITIZENSHIP.

OUGHT AND CONSTANT EFFORT OF OUR BEST MINDS AND OF OUR MOST

TIC AMERICANS ARE REQUIRED IN REVERSING THE TREND. THE JOB MUST

E FOR THIS NATION CAN LIVE AND GROW GREATER ONLY IF THE CHILDREN

S GENERATION ARE DEVELOPED INTO GOOD CITIZENS AND INTO SUITABLE

S FOR AMERICANS OF THE FUTURE.

K IT IS VERY COMMENDABLE THAT YOU WANTED TO MENTION THIS SITUATION

R PROGRAM OF ANYTHING THAT CAN BE DONE TO AROUSE PARENTS AND ADULTS

IR RESPONSIBILITIES TO AMERICANS OF THE FUTURE IS NOT ONLY DESIRABLE

GHLY NECESSARY. REGARDS. SINCERELY,

JOHN EDGAR HOOVER
DIRECTOR
FEDERAL BUREAU OF INVESTI-
GATION

TELEMETER   5:00PM   SLS.

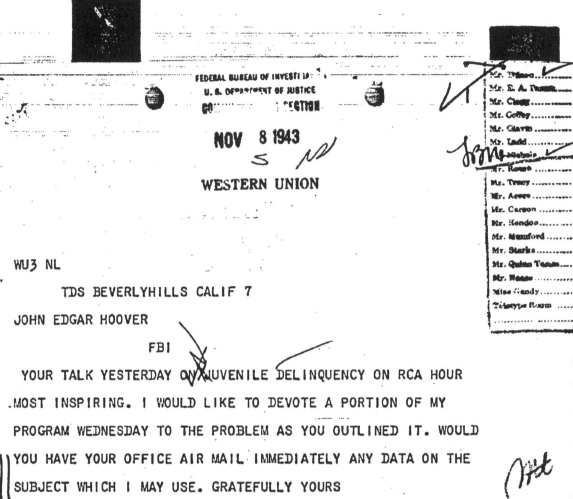

Mr. Tolson ✓
Mr. E. A. Tamm
Mr. Clegg
Mr. Coffey
Mr. Glavin
Mr. Ladd
Mr. Nichols ✓
Mr. Rosen
Mr. Tracy
Mr. Acers
Mr. Carson
Mr. Hendon
Mr. Mumford
Mr. Starke
Mr. Quinn Tamm
Mr. Nease
Miss Gandy
Teletype Room

WU3 NL

TDS BEVERLYHILLS CALIF 7

JOHN EDGAR HOOVER

        FBI

YOUR TALK YESTERDAY ON JUVENILE DELINQUENCY ON RCA HOUR

MOST INSPIRING. I WOULD LIKE TO DEVOTE A PORTION OF MY

PROGRAM WEDNESDAY TO THE PROBLEM AS YOU OUTLINED IT. WOULD

YOU HAVE YOUR OFFICE AIR MAIL IMMEDIATELY ANY DATA ON THE

SUBJECT WHICH I MAY USE. GRATEFULLY YOURS

EDDIE CANTOR   1012 NORTH ROXBURY DRIVE

BEVERLYHILLS.

        126AM.

RECORDED & INDEXED 1 62-

Wire to Los Angeles
11/9 8pm

33   NOV 11 1943

1012.

c.c. Mr. Nichols

April 29, 1944

Eddie Cantor
Waldorf Astoria Hotel
New York, New York

Dear Eddie:

I am returning herewith the letter addressed to
you under date of April 7, 1944, by Mr. Fred R. Levine of
Superior, Wisconsin, together with the newspaper clipping
accompanying Mr. Levine' letter and the carbon copy of
your answer to Mr. Levine' communication. Immediately
after you furnished this correspondence to me, I checked
into the matter within the Department of Justice to determine whether there was any way in which the statement charging you with equipping your automobile to use unrationed
butane gas might be retracted or alleviated. I have determined through my Los Angeles office that Mr. James T.
Harrington, Chief of the War Frauds Unit of the Department
of Justice, did not give out the press dispatch setting
forth the names of the persons, including yourself, who were
supposed to have this equipment. Mr. John Handy of the War
Production Board in Los Angeles advised several of the
persons named in the dispatch, after the story had appeared
in the papers, that if they would bring their automobiles to
the War Production Board in Los Angeles for inspection, in
order that it might be determined they did not have and never
had butane attachments on them, the War Production Board
would then issue a public retraction. I have not been able
to determine whether anyone has as yet taken his automobile
to the War Production Board for examination, but I would
suggest that if you have an automobile in the Los Angeles
area, you give consideration to taking this step, since,
I am advised as I have indicated, that the War Production
Board will then issue a statement retracting the previous

The Federal Bureau of Investigation has not parti-
cipated in any manner in the investigation of the case against

RECORDED 62-26544-7
F B I
INDEXED 27 MAY 4 1944

Tonker and consequently I am not in possession of any additional information concerning this phase of the matter.

If I can be of any further assistance to you, I hope that you will not hesitate to call upon me.

Sincerely,

J. Edgar Hoover

Attachments

GAS GADGET UNCOVERED

LOS ANGELES - (AP) - Charged with installing equipment in automobiles to permit use of unrationed butane gas instead of gasoline as fuel, Lawrence W. Zonker was named yesterday in a 10-count federal criminal information charging violation of War Production board regulations.

James T. Harrington, chief of the war frauds unit of the department of justice here, said Zonkers sold the equipment for as high as $1,000 per automobile to more than 40 motion picture actors and other wealthy Los Angeles citizens.

These included, Harrington said, Gary Cooper, Bob Hope, Eddie Cantor, L. B. Mayer; Producer William Goetz, Barbara Hutton, Carey Grant, and Director Henry Hathaway.

ENCLOSURE
62-26544-7

April 7, 1944

Dear Mr. Cantor:

The attached from the Duluth News Tribune of April 6, 1944.

Having in mind all the needed and apparent sincere war appeals made by you during your weekly radio program, I can hardly believe it.

Yours very truly,

(signed) Fred R. Lewis
Father of Two Naval Aviators
1403 No. 19th Street
Superior, Wisconsin

Mr. Eddie Cantor

Los Angeles, Calif.

1944 53

ENCLOSURE
62-26544-7

My dear _____:

     I am deeply grateful for your thoughtfulness in writing me. Most people condemn and criticize before actually checking on the facts. For your information, and for the others who were equally amazed and astounded, let me tell you that I never met Mr. Zonker - do not own any special equipment in my automobile to use Butane gas and have never been connected in this matter in any way, shape or form.

     Before I left Los Angeles, I was assured by James T. Harrington, Chief of the War Frauds Unit of the Dept. of Justice, that a statement of regret would be issued shortly.

     I hope it comes soon so that friendly people such as you can be reassured of my good faith in all matters that pertain to the welfare of our nation.

              Sincerely,

              Eddie Cantor

TO : DIRECTOR   DATE April 2, 1945

FROM : CLYDE TOLSON

SUBJECT :

Eddie Cantor telephoned and was referred to me. In connection with his Wednesday evening Ipana Toothpaste program, he is planning starting on Wednesday of this week, an essay contest to last four weeks for high school students. He states that he personally is planning to give war bonds for the best essays and awards to the high schools represented by the students who write the best essays on the subject "Juvenile Delinquency, Its Causes and Its Solution." He states that he has been in contact with Nicholas Murray Butler, of Columbia University, and with President Sproul, of UCLA, and he would like you as the third judge to go over the essays and select those which are deserving of awards. He states that he will have a California committee go over the essays and pick out the 25 best essays for final consideration by the judges.

I told Mr. Cantor that you are tremendously interested in juvenile delinquency and I felt that you would want to help him in his plan. I told him that I would present the matter to you and you would be in touch with him by telegram very soon.

RECORDED &
INDEXED

63- 26544 -8

APR 4 1945

39
57 APR 18 1945

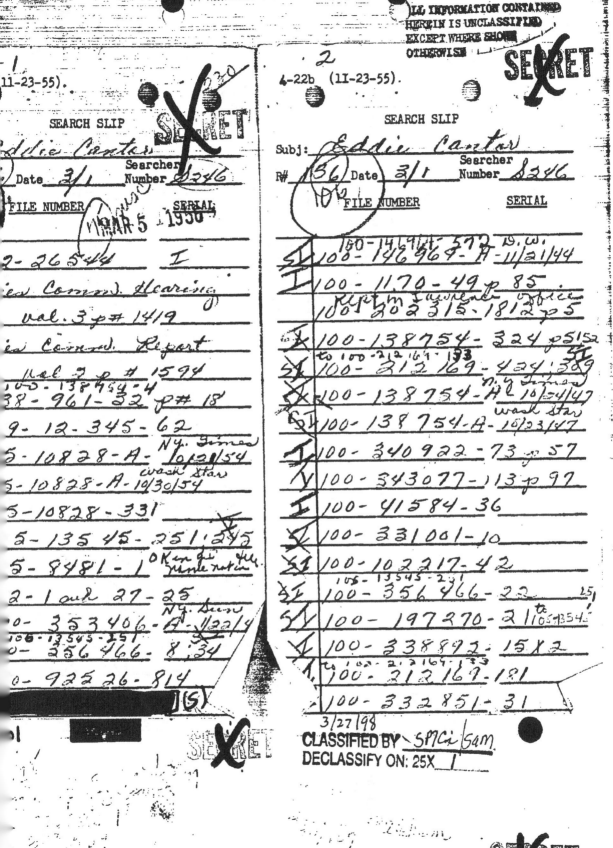

-1
(11-23-55).

2
4-22b (11-23-55).

SEARCH SLIP

Eddie Cantor

Date 3/1   Searcher Number 8246

FILE NUMBER   SERIAL

MAR 5 1958

2- 26544   I

ica Comm. Hearing
    vol. 3 p# 1419

ica Comm. Report
    vol 7 p # 1594
100-138754-4
38- 961- 32 p# 18
9- 12- 345- 62
5- 10828- A- N.Y. Times 10/21/54
5- 10828- A- Wash Star 10/30/54
5- 10828- 331
5- 135 45- 251:245
5- 8481- 1 OK enumeration
2- 1 and 27- 25
0- 353406- A- N.Y. Sun 1/22/4
100-13545-251
0- 256 466- 8:34
0- 925 26- 814

(S)

SECRET

SEARCH SLIP

Subj: Eddie Cantor

R# 156 Date 3/1   Searcher Number 8246

FILE NUMBER   SERIAL

100- 146 969- 577 D.W.
100- 146 969- A- 11/21/44
100- 1170- 49 p 85
100- 202 315- 1812 p 5
100- 138754- 324 p515
  to 100-212 169-133
100- 212 169- 424:309
100- 138 754- A 10/=4/47 N.Y. Times
100- 138 754- A- 10/23/47 Wash Star
100- 340 922- 73 p 57
100- 343 077- 113 p 97
100- 41584- 36
100- 331 001- 10
100- 102 217- 42
  105-13545-251
100- 356 466- 22   25
100- 197 270- 21 to 10/11354
100- 338 892- 15 X 2
  100-212 169-133
100- 212 169- 181
100- 332 851- 31

3/27/98
CLASSIFIED BY SMCi/sam
DECLASSIFY ON: 25X 1

SECRET

3
4-22b (11-23-55)

SEARCH SLIP

Subj: Eddie Cantor

R# 156 Date 3/1 Searcher Number 8246

FILE NUMBER	SERIAL
100-7061-923-	
100-7061-420	
Kept in Lawrence office	
100-202315-919 p 49,	
51, 52, 56	
To 100-391042	
100-138759-4 p 118,120	
100-181338-30	
100-138754-459, 146	
to 100-138754-2 v 10-24-47	
100-138754-308 p42	
100-348418-7 p 9	
100-138754-367 p36	
100-141610-4	
to 353406-2 NY Syn 1-22-43	
100-353406-4	
100-0-27010	
100-138754-A NY times N.Y. Times	
100-138754-H-10/20/47	
100-17242-14	
100-15252-39 p 403	
100-391042-21 p 14	
100-337779-121 3	

4
4-22b (11-23-55)

SEARCH SLIP

Subj: Eddie Cantor

R# 156 Date 3/1 Searcher Number 8246

FILE NUMBER	SERIAL
100-356466-147 p	
100-138754-A-10/3 B.W.	
100-138754-865	
100-383693-2	
100-297187-15	
100-344922-7	
100-103141-11	
100-353979-22	
100-391042-21	
100-6633-2	
to 100-184445	
100-184445-14 p1	
to 105-13545-251	
100-356466-6	
100-370750-127	
100-79718-14	
to 100-138754-A NY to 24-47 Chicago	
100-138754-H-1111	
Kept in Lawrence off.	
100-202315-787	
100-202315-58	
100-92526-993	
100-168670-25 p	

(1-23-55)

6

4-22b (11-23-55)

SEARCH SLIP

Subj: *Eddie Cantor*

Date 3/1   Searcher Number S246

FILE NUMBER	SERIAL
0-138754-	990
0-123567-	556
0-332879-	7; 8
0-47900-	14
-138754-	571 p 26
-184445-	30 p 32
-138754-	691 p 36
-138754-	516 ; 500
-51620-	14
0-352479-	5
-138754-	11/9/47 the worker
-138754-	362 p 527
-138754-	67
-32820-	205
-235432-	13
-338892-	L
-212169-	155
-405766-	5 5

SEARCH SLIP

Subj: *Eddie Cantor*

R# 156   Date 3/1   Searcher Number S246

FILE NUMBER	SERIAL
100-414973-	5 p 18
100-370691-	20 p 11
100-338712-	17
100-352560-	7
100-138754-A	10/23/47 N.Y. times N.W.
100-225072-A	9/4/43 the worker
100-138754-A	11/2/47
100-184445-A	6/29/43 D.W.
100-225072-A	7/6/43 D.W.
100-225072-A	8/30/43 D.W.
100-155425-L	n.y. times
100-225072-A	6/28/43
100-2143-26	65-33716-29
100-138754-A	10/25/47 wash star
100-355869-2	
100-242224-2	
100-138754-A	10/27/47 wash post
100-344437-5	
100-138754-504	6

7

4-22b (11-23-55).

8

4-22b (11-23-55).

SEARCH SLIP

Subj: *Eddie Cantor*

R# 106   Date 3/1   Searcher Number S 246

	FILE NUMBER	SERIAL
L	100-10123-114 p 1092	B
I	100-71095-3	
S	100-39336-A Hollywood J.	-A 4/27/50
L	101-2525-142 p 23	
L	61-777-3- Baltimore Sun. 1/31/46	
I	61-7341-5-22	
L	44-25-34	
I	62-43818-827; 832; 833; 854; 839	
I	62-79208-3	
I	62-71694-8	
I	94-37546-10	
LDG	65-56402-1 -2761X16	
ND	94-1-196-180	
ND	65-62469-9	
I	61-7562-A- D.W. 4/8/44	
I	61-7582-1298 p 482	
I	61-7566-24 tol 13875	

SEARCH SLIP

Subj: *Eddie Cantor*

R# 336   Date 3/1   Searcher Number S 24
106

	FILE NUMBER	SERIAL
S	61-7561-247; 33; 391047 254 X 20	
I	61-7560-339; 333 367; 717	
S	62-77586-9	
S	61-7562-331 X 36	
I	61-9358-2	
I	65-58190-43	
I	62-43818-1015	
I	62-77586-9 p 2	
I	94-3-4 sub 1115-5 X 14	
I	2-1004-205	
I	62-43818-1022	
S	54-717-5	
I	65-33716-57; 20	
I	39-2258-323; 21	
S	62-12188-1323; 1209	

(11-23-55) SECRET   4-22b (11-23-55)

SEARCH SLIP   SEARCH SLIP

Eddie Cantor   Subj. **Eddie Cantor**

Date 3/1   Searcher Number *8246*   R# (15) Date 3/1   Searcher Number *8246*

FILE NUMBER	SERIAL		FILE NUMBER	SERIAL
2 - 43818 - 1000			100 - 342972 - 958	
62 - 26544 - 7		MD	94 - 35690 - 3 ; MD	
94 - 4 - 5519 - 5	T	I	100 - 56674 - 1190 p 137	
to 65-58106-462		SI	100 - 37226 - 310	
5 - 58700 - 347; 1665		MD	94 - 1 sub 5576 - 139	
1 - 9218 - 16		MD	94 - 4 - 4169 - 3	
2 - 78312 - 2 p 12		MD	94 - 6 - 5832	
94 - 1 - 22773 - 22		SI	61 - 7559 - 3951 X	
77 - 14177 - 27			61 - 7558 - 92	
1 - 10149 - 810 p 4			61 - 7566 - 1633	
94 - 4 - 2695 - 36		I	100 - 356137 - 677	
1 - 7559 - 3136 p 3;		I	100 - 184489 - 5	
62-77586 -9 2122			to 100 - 338892 - 17	
		X	100 - 338892 - 45 p 8; 44	
5 - 33716 - 29			100 - 338947 - 2	
2 - 43818 - 822	SI		100 - 243765 - 8	
777 - 26 - 118; 90		I	100 - 351780 - 27	
2 - 875 - 424 p 23			IA-18-445 30	
1 - 5381 - 1727		SI	100 - 71095 - 22	
2 - 108 - 5455	9	SI	100 - 138754 - 973	10

4-22b. (11-23-55)

SEARCH SLIP

Subj: *Eddie Cantor*

R# 156   Date 3/1   Searcher Number S246

FILE NUMBER	SERIAL
100-37226-334	
100-272700-7 p30 part 1	
100-212169-672 p19	
100-295492-19	
100-146964-572; 745	
100-338.892-17	
100-7061-923; 631	
65-59184-107	
65-62926-1423	
100-37226-236	
61-8381-618X p305	
8-1004-215; 216; 228	
65-4279-968 p6	
100-212169-A-10/8/47	
97-3866-26	
100-353384-A-5/21/49	
100-339703-19	
100-212169-664 p4/11	

4-22b. (11-23-55)

SEARCH SLIP

Subj: *Eddie Cantor*

R# 156   Date 3/1   Searcher Number S246

FILE NUMBER	SERIAL
65-57711-8 p34	
65-58700-462	
68-65699-1	
97-2866-15	
100-66569-4	
100-351006-3 p389	
100-225072-1, 2	
100-212169-133; 159	
100-340922-A-9/7/5	
100-353433-A-4/27/5	
100-37226-409	
121-1429-37 p6	
61-7560-1675	
61-10149-666	
102-1-31-21	
100-3-36-287; 319	
100-122008-11	

13

2b, (11-23-55)

SEARCH SLIP

Eddie Cantor

(5b) Date __3/1__ Searcher Number *8246*

FILE NUMBER   **SERIAL**

Eddie, (Mrs)

100-331001-10   b1

~~████████████~~ (B)

105-13545-251

Eddie Cantor Show

94-4-2439-139

Eddy

100-92526-922

100-356466-161

131-29773-7

62-100521-1

62-44129-4

approx. 100 Ones not

listed

P.

64-1505-19-8   *15*

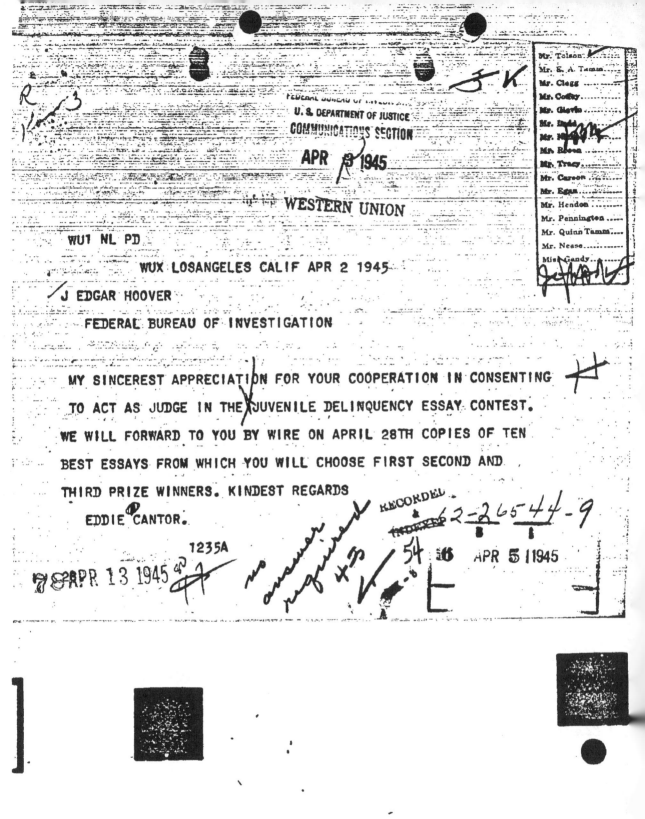

WESTERN UNION

WU1 NL PD

WUX LOSANGELES CALIF APR 2 1945

J EDGAR HOOVER

FEDERAL BUREAU OF INVESTIGATION

MY SINCEREST APPRECIATION FOR YOUR COOPERATION IN CONSENTING

TO ACT AS JUDGE IN THE JUVENILE DELINQUENCY ESSAY CONTEST.

WE WILL FORWARD TO YOU BY WIRE ON APRIL 28TH COPIES OF TEN

BEST ESSAYS FROM WHICH YOU WILL CHOOSE FIRST SECOND AND

THIRD PRIZE WINNERS. KINDEST REGARDS

EDDIE CANTOR.

1235A

RECORDED

62-26544-9

APR 13 1945

APR 5 11945

April 16, 1945

GMM:vhm

Mr. Eddie Cantor
1012 North Roxbury Drive
Beverly Hills, California

Dear Eddie:

I thought you would be interested
in the enclosed letter and juvenile delinquency
essay received from Miss Ruby Tatum of Elizabethtown, North Carolina. Receipt of this manuscript
has been acknowledged to Miss Tatum and I have
told her that it was being forwarded to you.

With best wishes and kind regards,

Sincerely yours,

J. Edgar Hoover

Enclosure

le 4-10-45 and essay received from Ruby Tatum.

CMN:vhm

April 16, 1945

Miss Ruby Tatum
Rural Free Delivery
   Route 2, Box 74
Elizabethtown, North Carolina

Dear Miss Tatum:

      I wish to thank you for your letter of April 10, 1945, enclosing your essay on juvenile delinquency. It has been read with interest but I am not in a position to comment upon it at this time. The manuscript is being forwarded to Mr. Eddie Canter, sponsor of the contest, so that all of the judges will have an opportunity to read it.

                Sincerely yours,

                J. Edgar Hoover

                John Edgar Hoover
                Director

Mr. E. A. Tamm
Mr. Clegg
Mr. Coffey
Mr. Glavin
Mr. Ladd ✓
Mr. Nichols
Mr. Rosen
Mr. Tracy
Mr. Carson
Mr. Egan
Mr. Hendon
Mr. Pennington
Mr. Quinn Tamm
Mr. Nease
Miss Gandy

WESTERN UNION

WU1 NL PD

WUX LOSANGELES CALIF APR 24 1945

J EDGAR HOOVER

FEDERAL BUREAU OF INV

WE ARE MAILING TO YOU TONIGHT THE JUVENILE DELINQUENCY
ESSAYS OF THE TEN FINALISTS WHOSE COMPOSITIONS HAVE BEEN
SELECTED FROM THE THOUSANDS SUBMITTED BY OUR PRELIMINARY
STAFF. THE ESSAYS AS YOU RECEIVE THEM WILL NOT BEAR THE NAMES
OF THEIR AUTHORS BUT EACH WILL HAVE A KEY LETTER IN THE
UPPER LEFT HAND CORNER. WE ASK YOU TO SELECT FROM THIS GROUP
A FIRST PRIZE WINNER, A SECOND AND THIRD. IT WILL NOT BE
NECESSARY FOR YOU TO RETURN THESE ESSAYS BUT MERELY TO
TELEGRAPH ME, AS SOON AS ABSOLUTELY POSSIBLE YOUR SELECTIONS
IN THIS MANNER: SHOULD YOU SELECT ESSAY "B" AS FIRST WINNER,
ESSAY "D" AS SECOND WINNER AND ESSAY "F" AS THIRD WINNER,
MERELY CONVEY THOSE SELECTIONS TO US BY WIRING ME COLLECT:
B --1, D -- 2, F -- 3. SIMILAR COPIES ARE IN THE HANDS OF
OUR OTHER JUDGES. SINCE WE ARE TO MAKE THE ANNOUNCEMENT OF
THE WINNERS WEDNESDAY MAY 2ND IT IS MOST IMPORTANT THAT
WE HAVE YOUR SELECTIONS NOT LATER THAN TUESDAY MORNING MAY
FIRST. WE KNOW THAT THIS WILL CROWD YOU A BIT BUT THE
SELECTION OF THE FINALISTS WAS A TREMENDOUS TASK AND WE DID
NOT WANT TO CLOSE THE CONTEST BEFORE EVERY OPPORTUNITY HAD
BEEN GIVEN TO THE WRITER TO GET HIS ESSAY TO US. MY
SINCEREST THANKS FOR YOUR GRAND COOPERATION.

EDDIE CANTOR 1012 N ROXBURY DR BEVERLY HILLS CALIF.

RECORDED 62-26544-12
FBI
MAY 2 1945

Nichols 4-28-45 EDM

28-45 EDM

1259A

cc: Mr Nichols

B D F B 1 D 2 F 3 2 1012 N.

URGENT-COLLECT

To: COMMUNICATIONS SECTION

Transmit the following message to: APRIL 30, 1945

62-26544-12

MR. EDDIE CANTOR
1012 NORTH ROXBURY DRIVE
BEVERLY HILLS, CALIFORNIA

EX-4

ESSAYS WERE SPLENDID. MY PERSONAL CHOICE: A —1, I —2, D —3.
PLEASE GIVE MY PERSONAL CONGRATULATIONS TO THE WINNERS.

JOHN EDGAR HOOVER, DIRECTOR, FEDERAL BUREAU OF INVESTIGATION.

Tolson
E. A. Tamm
Clegg
Coffey
Glavin
Ladd
Nichols
Rosen
Tracy
Mohr
Carson
Hendon
Mumford
Jones
Quinn Tamm
Nease
Miss Gandy

COPIES DESTROYED
270 AUG 11 1964

50 MAY 14 1945

FEDERAL BUREAU OF INVESTIGATION
U. S. DEPARTMENT OF JUSTICE
COMMUNICATIONS SECTION

APR 30 1945

SENT VIA WESTERN UNION   557 M   Per _____

INITIALED IN
DIRECTOR'S OFFICE

Dear Sirs:

I am a High School girl, 16 years old.

I am submitting my ideas on the subject of Juvenile Delinquence, to your contest.

Eddie Cantoe

My Mother is deeply interested in this particular subject, as she has had expierences with children who have needed a friend and turned to her, rather than to their own parents.

Therefore my ideas are based on facts I've learned from her experiences and from my associations with children who have expressed the great desire that their Parents were as understanding as mine, and that they could talk to their Parents as I can.

I feel sorry for these children, it is sympathetic and something should be done about it.

I do not know the address to which the contest themes were to be sent, so I'm sending mine to Mr J. Edgar Hoover, of the F.B.I. as I was told he was to be one of the Judges.

Hopeing my theme will be of interest to you;

      I am, Yours very truly

              b7C

        Sweetwater, Texas

RECORDED & INDEXED

EX-60 21 MAY 3 1945

1 ENCL

April 30, 1945

Sweetwater, Texas

Dear Miss Oldham:

I wish to acknowledge your letter postmarked April 23, 1945, enclosing a copy of the essay which you prepared on the subject of juvenile delinquency. This manuscript reached me after the contest sponsored by Mr. Eddie Cantor had been concluded and I am returning it to you.

Your interest in this problem is very much appreciated by me and I am sending some material which it is believed you may care to read.

Sincerely yours,

J. Edgar Hoover

John Edgar Hoover
Director

Enclosure

Our Duty to Youth
Treason in Amer Home
Amer of Tomorrow

FEDERAL BUREAU OF INVESTIGATION
U. S. DEPARTMENT OF JUSTICE
COMMUNICATIONS SECTION

MAY 9 1945

TELEMETER

FROM LOSA1 9 10-34 AM

CTOR   IMMEDIATE ~~~~ ATTENTION MR. J. J. MC QUIRE.

CANTOR SHOW SCRIPT BEING REVISED AND WILL NOT BE AVAILABLE

AN HOUR. WILL PHONE SOON AS I GET IT. STATIONSIKKI LOS

ELES AND KFSD SAN DIEGO WILL CARRY BROADCAST AT SIX P.M.

62-26544-14

F B I

RECORDED 29 MAY 12 1945

23 1945   EX 33

U. S. DEPARTMENT OF JUSTICE
COMMUNICATIONS SECTION

MAY J 1945

WESTERN UNION

WU3 NL PD

WUX LOSANGELES CALIF MAY 8 1945

EDGAR HOOVER

FED BUR OF INV

DEAR EDGAR: WANT TO THANK YOU FOR YOUR COOPERATION IN JUDGING

JUVENILE DELINQUENCY ESSAY CONTEST. IN TRIBUTE TO YOU AM

DOING A BROADCAST REVOLVING AROUND ■■ YOUR HAVING MADE ME AN

HONORARY G-MAN. DONT GET FRIGHTENED. THIS IS ALL IN A

DREAM BECAUSE A GUY WHO'S AFRAID OF IDA CERTAINLY DOESNT

BELONG IN THE FBI. WARMEST REGARDS

EDDIE.

162-26544-15

RECORDED 6A F B I

29 MAY 12 1945

EX-23

cc: Mr Nichols

ffice Memorandum • UNITED STATES GOVERNMENT

DW

    MR. TOLSON   DATE: 5/11/45

  : R. C. HENDON

CT: EDDIE CANTOR BROADCAST

Mr. Tolson
Mr. E. A. Tamm
Mr. Clegg
Mr. Coffey
Mr. Glavin
Mr. Ladd
Mr. Nichols
Mr. Rosen
Mr. Tracy
Mr. Carson
Mr. Egan
Mr. Hendon
Mr. Pennington
Mr. Quinn Tamm
Tele. Room
Mr. Nease
Miss Beahm
Miss Gandy

    As a matter of record, the Young and Rubicam Agency
ling the Eddie Cantor script contacted Mr. Ellsworth of our
Angeles Office on May 9, 1945 and advised that they were
ing on the script for the broadcast that evening which
t with the work of the Bureau. Mr. Ellsworth stated that
derstood the script would be built around the Director having
Eddie Cantor a Special Agent badge and made him an honorary
.

    Pursuant to my instructions, Mr. Ellsworth advised them that
was objectionable inasmuch as we had numerous requests for
ary badges which policy and the law would not permit. It was
ted out that should such a reference be made on Cantor's broadcast
uld possibly receive many more requests and individuals who were
ting us from day to day would misconstrue and misunderstand such
ences and would not be able to figure out why they too did not
ve honorary badges. Mr. Ellsworth was also instructed to obtain
y of the script so that we could make any other necessary sug-
ons. He was not able to get the script until approximately three
 before the broadcast started. He telephoned it in and sugges—
 were made just before 7:00 p.m. for certain changes to eliminate
ences to our having furnished Cantor a badge, to eliminate ref-
es to our handling black market matters, a reference to the
 third degree and similar objectionable passages. It was under-
 that Young and Rubicam were very receptive to these suggestions
ecessary changes were made so that the broadcast was finally
factory.

a letter was sent to Cantor

RECORDED

29 MAY 12 1945

FBI

EX - 23

EX - 2

Y 2 3 1945

E.   It's the Sal Hapatica commercial program, and there's the
opening music and so forth. Then Vonsell says:

"Ladies and gentlemen we turn the clock back to last night,
and we find our hero, Eddie Cantor, at his home in lounging robe and
pajamas, having retired to his quarters and having counted his
quarters he is preparing to go to bed."

Then the whole program deals with his about to become a
G-man, or the fact that he might become a G-man, and a dream of his
that he goes out and breaks up a black market ring. He awakens at
the end of the thing by someone ~~pinning~~ his badge into the seat of
his nightshirt. That's the general type of the program. It deals
with the FBI and his being a detective.

Maurice: Mr. Cantor, isn't it past your bed time?

Cantor: I know, Maurice, but I'm so excited I can't sleep. Imagine
J. Edgar Hoover sending me a ~~badge~~ letter. First thing you know, he'll be
making me a G-man. Isn't that exciting!

M.   I do think it's exciting, Mr. Cantor, but how long do I have
to be strapped in this chair with that sun lamp shining in my face?

C.   I'm just practicing, Maurice. After all, you never know
when I may have to third degree someone. At least you could be a
good sport about it.

M.   I don't mind being a good sport, Mr. Cantor, ~~but~~ how many
times are you going to keep asking me what did I do with Hitler's body?

Oh, all right. And you're free now. Will you get me a
of warm milk before I go to bed please?

But you've had five glasses of milk already.

I don't care. I've got something to celebrate-tonight I'm
to get homoginized.

Very good, sir.

The door opens and closes.

Gosh, I think I might become a G-man. I wonder, 'Does that
le me to more gasoline?' ~~Kut~~ my franarl to Frank Seastra,

Door opens

Hello, Harry.

Hello, Eddie. I got your message to come right over. What's

What's up? Look at this badge. My pal, J. Edgar Hoover,
make me a G-man someday. And not only that, I had lunch with
esterday and he let me fool around with his handcuffs.
rressed) You should have seen me. Before I knew it I had myself
uffed to the leg of the table.

You handcuffed youself to the leg of the table? That was
y dumb.

I'll say it was dumb. When Mr. Hoover had to pick up the
I felt terrible.

I can imagine. When it comes to handing out money, you've
s been handcuffed.

Harry, what do you mean by that remark?

Here there are several pages of incident.

- 2 -

BEGinning on page 5 of the script.

C.   Why, Leonard _____. Hello, Leonard. Leonard, ~~Irwanted~~
the reason I wanted you to hurry over is that I wanted you to read
this letter I got from J. Edgar Hoover.

L.   Oh, holy smokes! Do you mean to read this letter, I put
down Forever Amber?

C.   Leonard, you were reading Forever Amber?

L.   Sure. I've read it twice already.

V.   You mean to say you're reading Forever Amber for the third
time?

C.   You must like that book.

L.   I sure do. What's it about, Mr. Cantor?

C.   Oh, fine. What's it about, Leonard?

L.   Yeah.

C.   Well, have you ever read Tom ~~Pryor~~ Sawyer

L.   No.

C.   Fine. You lend me your copy of Forever Amber and I'll lend
you Tom ~~Pryor~~ Sawyer

L.   Well, I don't know. What's it about?

C.   It's about a little barefoot boy.

L.   Barefoot? That's risque. I'll just stick to Forever Amber.

C.   All right, Leonard. But, say, what would you think if J.
Edgar Hoover made me a G-man?

L.   Oh boy! A G-man. Say, Mr. Cantor, I could be your assistant.
My uncle is with the FBI.

C.   Your uncle with the FBI.

L.   Yeah. They picked him up in Mexico.

- 3 -

Oh, forget your uncle. What's makes you think you could be
a detective?

Well, when I go to see a mystery picture all's I have to do
watch five minutes of it and I can tell you which one is the murderer.

How are you able to do that?

I come in at the end of the picture.

Baby cries out.

What's that?

My kid. I left him in in the next room when I came over.

Well, let's go get him. It was Eddie Cantor Vonsell, Jr.
I wanted to show the badge to.

Door opens

Hello, there, little fellow. Look at the badge your Uncle
Eddie's got. What do you think of that? Your Uncle Eddie a G-Man.

Gurgle.

He's trying to talk. Since he's been listening to the radio
talks much better.

Xkasgagagax Oog oog

Isn't that wonderful?

Wonderful? What's xkasgagagax oog oog?

That's googoo spelled backwards.

That's perfectly natural. He has a backward father. Look,
trying to reach for my badge. I wonder what he's thinking about.

Googoo. Popeye says he's a G-man. How bould he ever get his

He's been married 31 years and he can't even get his boy. When he
showed me his G-man badge, he was so proud, He threw out his chest so
that almost touched his shirt. Some physique. At his age, a detective.

- 4 -

He sure will look funny speeding down the street with a siren on his wheelchair. Still, if I were a criminal I would hate to have popeye looking for my hideout. Gosh, he could stand on a corner and send his eyes around the block.

C.   Harry, while You're here in my house I'd like you to hear this record Freddie Martel made.

V.   Well, Eddie, I'd like to hear it but really I've got to get the baby home, and besides I want to write J. Edgar Hoover and see if I can get an *a real* FBI badge.

C.   Harry, what makes you think he'd give you an FBI badge.

V.   Well, after all I've helped G-men all over the country.

C.   Harry, what kind of G-men have you helped?

V.   The kind of men that wake up in the morning in need of a laxative and say, 'Gee I feel headachy. Gee, I feel dull. Gee, I wish I didn't have to get up.'

C.   Oh. And I suppose you help them by telling them if they want to feel better faster they should take a glass of sparkling Sal Hepatica.

V.   That's right.

C.   How do you like that? I just became an FBI man today and from that little *clue* you gave I figured out what it was. Aren't I smart?

        THEN THEY GO INTO A COMMERCIAL FOR SEVERAL PAGES.
        BEGINNING ON PAGE THIRTEEN IT SAYS:

Maurice. Mr. Cantor, everyone has gone home. Do you think you ought to try to get some sleep?

C.   I'll try, Maurice, but I'm so excited about my badge.

M.   Before you retire sir, let's have a go at those wrinkles.

- 5 -

Lightning Source UK Ltd.
Milton Keynes UK
UKOW06f0754251114

242139UK00010B/338/P